Yes God, I'm listening!

Dr. Shanta Barton-Stubbs

Dr. Shanta Barton-Stubbs

Cover illustration: Reginald Simmons –
photo credit

Published by Under Construction
Empowerment Services, LLC.

214 South Parramoreave.

Orlando, Fl 32805

ISBN:099732970X

Printed in the United States of America

Dedication

I dedicate this book to all who made it possible for me to see beyond the natural. To my mom and dad for always being that support team I needed during the rough days of completing my dissertation. Knowing my worth when I couldn't see it and teaching me the life skills which I utilize today. To Sheaneaka and Leamon my siblings for being my silent cheerleaders since forever, and allowing me to be me. To Reggie for pushing me to be my best and the person who sits in the background while I speak to audiences and motions me to smile more, talk louder and cut it shorter. Thank you for being the person who had me 100% and would say "put on your heels today, they'll take you more serious." To Zacheriah, Jalia and Shakia for teaching me how to love beyond the norm.Most importantly to the New Image

Dr. Shanta Barton-Stubbs
Youth Center family, for making me be better, in order to lead by example.

Thank you Bruce and Kathy Carlson for teaching me how to have faith. Your acts of kindness will never be forgotten.

Table of Contents

Introduction

Hi there!

Thank you for taking the time to read 'Yes, God I am listening, my personal lessons on my walk with God. This book comprises of various subjects and topics which you will find are related in a particular way to the teachings from the duration of the courses I attended while completing my dissertation in Christian Theology. Each story and topic I have covered in this book discusses the word of God in a unique way as I have also added my own personal experience to the book.

In **Genesis 3:8**, we read about how Adam and Eve shared a certain 'walking' relationship with God where we also understand that God created man only to enjoy a mutual relationship which involved sharing space and companionship.

Once again in the **Book of Genesis 4:26**, we observe that though mankind began calling on the name of the Lord from the earliest of days, Enoch was one of the first person written about in the Bible who discovered the joy of walking with God and hence he was blessed with the joy of being taken to Paradise.

Using the example of Enoch, we continue to witness on a daily basis the passion of people wanting to experience God by walking with him through prayer. In our walk with God, we get a better understanding of the scriptures through the wisdom of the Holy Spirit and the revelation of the glory of God.

If you spend time around any Christian, you will soon find or hear a common phrase from them often, that of having a meaningful relationship with God. I cover this topic on Faith in my book.

The various writings and stories you will come across in this book mainly deal with how things are handled and how they can be dealt with after being exposed to the appropriate scriptures as mentioned in the Holy Book. After all, the Bible does work as a guide for us to use the verses and the many learning points to be applied to our daily lives.

After my time dedicated to my studies, my focus on the curriculum and the different topics taught there have assisted me in my own walk with God.

You will come across several segments in this book which are written to inspire and encourage the lives of several others by promoting the love and mercy of God and understanding how his holy word works magically for us in our lives without us even realizing it.

Yes God, I'm Listening!

I have compiled this book as my own personal mission to share the joy I have felt on my walk with God with other individuals and how to live their life in the best possible way as recommended in the word of God; the Holy Bible.

With the knowledge and understanding I have received after attending the course at the International Miracle Institute, I have discovered that we bring about several illnesses upon ourselves by not reaching out to God through his scriptures which should work as our guiding light.

I do intend on continuing my 'walk with God' and also help others who are struggling to reach out to God instead of giving up so easily. With this book I feel empowered enough to reach out to people who are eager to know more about God and reach out to him not just in times of need but always know that he is there and all we need to do is wait patiently.

We will always be faced with hurdles and stop signs along our way but at the end of the day we should remember this; With God all things are possible and can be done with no fear whatsoever. Please forward to more to come. I know this is only the beginning to what's in store.

Chapter 1: Building your Faith in God

1 Timothy 4:12 says, *"Do not let anyone look down upon you because you are young, but set an example for the believers in your speech, conduct, in love, in faith and in purity."*

Whenever we plan a road trip, we always look up a map for the route, don't we? Along with planning a route, we also put in all our faith and trust in the person driving to get us to our destination safe and sound.

We do not plan for any hurdles but we do prepare ourselves mentally and physically to be prepared for any obstacles which cross our way during the road trip. Similarly, when we consider and make a decision to walk with God, our first priority should be to put our faith in him without giving it a second thought.

We should not fear anything as long as we believe, and when you believe, you can expect nothing short of miracles to happen.

Building your faith takes a while especially when you get questioned time and again about your faith in a person you have never actually seen. Faith in God speaks about how we rely on him completely and wholly. When you have faith in God, you accept every decision of his which becomes a part of your life.

God understands what you want and what you need. However, we always consider ourselves to be wiser and think that we know what we need. When God answers your prayers, it is his way of telling you and providing you with what he knows is what you need at that point in time.

Several times in the scriptures, God provides us with a way, however, we tend to question that way with human logic. In **Mark Chapter 10: Verse43** the scriptures read as, *"Whoever amongst you wants to be a leader must also be your servant."*

Several people are unable to comprehend what that verse means or refers to, the verse states that if you want to be great and accomplish greater things, you must learn to serve those who need to be served or assisted. We often look down upon serving others and instead prefer to be served.

In serving others, we are enriching our experience of walking with God. By this statement what I am trying to convey is that we need to trust God in what he views as greatness and not what we as humans think about what being great is all about.

We need to rely and trust in God's understanding and what it means for us rather than trying to reach a conclusion ourselves on our interpretation of what the scripture means to us.

Faith in God gets difficult for us to acknowledge and accept especially during tough times in our lives. This is what the key point of understanding faith is all about; knowing and applying the wisdom of having faith in all the situations you face in your life.

I am very sure there are several of us who are unable to grasp the concept of faith well enough to hold back our negative thoughts when confronted with trials and tribulations.

Our faith needs to be strong enough to accept whatever comes our way and know that God keeps his promises to us of protecting and safeguarding us no matter what we face in our lives.

God has proven to us that he keeps his promises as mentioned in **Hebrews 10:23**, so therefore our faith shall remain strong, that he will do what he knows to be best for us.

In my own life, there have been several instances when my faith has been shaken, while I have felt hopeful, but being hopeful does not mean having faith.

When we talk about faith, what we are implying is to let the situation unfold as per God's plan. Being hopeful means that you are still doubtful about what is going to be the outcome of the hurdle you are being confronted with.

Hope leads us to have some uncertainty, but also gives us something to hold on too, wishing for a certain outcome.

While I am a Christian and I practice the teachings as preached in the Holy Scriptures, I have to confess that somewhere along this way I assumed it to be alright to be hopeful for something rather than believing that it would happen accordingly to how God see fit.

The Human Mindset and Believing in God

This hopeful mindset was created when God decided not to side with me and answer my prayers accordingly how I felt necessary. This thought also came about when I understood that there will be times when God's will, will be done and there will be times when his will may not be the will that I wanted or expected to happen.

So being human and with my human mindset, I assumed that maybe, just maybe if I believed hard enough and hoped long enough that I may just receive what I am asking (and in some cases, almost pleading) for. I can however surely vouch for the fact that I am not the only one who has been hopeful most of the time.

We always hope that our family members or friends will begin to follow the teachings of

Christ, and take the right path. We hope that our life will get better soon or later. We hope for several other things, but in reality we know that at the end of the day whatever happens will be done in accordance with God's will and not what we hope or wish for.

When we do not know what beholds us in the future and we are unsure of what lies ahead, we are left with uncertainty since we do not know what to expect from a problem that lies ahead of us. We can only hope and wish that the outcome of the situation favors us or at least the outcome is suitable to our liking.

When we talk about faith we are basing the idea that no matter what the outcome is, we accept it gracefully as the will of God and that it works for the better. It is an idea that is based more on spirituality than hope, because then we are assuming that there is a certain force at work which will account for all the actions and situations which occur in our lives.

No matter what the eventual outcome of the situation is, faith works only if the believer has full confidence and does not get hesitant during the times of trials being faced. The believer has to be assured that whatever the decision or the outcome is, it is done in his or her best interest.

The Difference between Hope and Faith

While we are discussing the topic of Hope and Faith and before I begin to explain what the difference is between both of them, I would like to share a story of mine which happened in 2005.

I was planning a fundraiser event for my non-profit organization which required over

$7,000 to plan and execute. I began the project without taking into consideration the cost it was going to be to me and the organization, but I was already far into the project to step back or put the entire event on hold till the funds came in.

However, once the deadline started getting closer, I did begin to feel the nervous pangs everyday since I was still almost $5,000 under budget.

I was then invited to attend a meeting with a person I had complete trust in and considered to be my advisor. At the meeting he approached the subject about the event and how my arrangements were going and what was my plan for the event.

Since I was so stressed with the deadline approaching, I never took it into consideration that this was the path that God intended me to use. I quickly shared my fear with my advisor about how I was not sure about how I could organize the event completely without the sufficient funds required. But while sharing my misery and doubts I did share with my advisor that I was hopeful about the entire event being successfully carried out.

While I have been nervous on several other occasions I was in particular concerned about how everything would work and to be very honest I was not 100% sure that I would be able to make things work within the limited funds I had for the event. But for some strange reason, I refused to cancel the event.

There was a tiny part of me which continued to have faith in myself that I could pull this off no matter what the situation. Although I am very sure if somebody had to measure the amount of faith I had, it would probably be the size of a mustard seed.

There was no way I could fail or give up on this event at that point in time because I was already in too deep and walking out of it would affect several others as well. During this period of duress I continued speaking with my friend and advisor about the event till I received a phone call from him one evening informing me that he was willing to loan me the balance amount for me to successfully organize the event and that I could pay him back once the event was done.

The project, i.e. the event was being organized to raise funds for a summer camp with the non-profit organization I had started. So technically that meant that I needed to raise more than enough funds from the fund raiser event to not only pay back the loan amount to my friend but also have sufficient funds left with me to use for the summer camp in order for it to run successfully.

The fundraiser event was successful, however, I only manage to raise enough funds for the amount I had spent on the event and I had to repay the loan given to me to have the event.

As I got my cashier's check ready to be given to my advisor, I felt the same nervous pangs all over again. I was scared and very afraid. Mainly because I had absolutely no clue what I would do for the summer camp once the loan amount was returned.

Matthew Chapter 17, Verse 20 states, *"Because you have so little faith. Truly I say to you, if you have faith as small as a mustard seed, you can say to this mountain, "Move from here to there," and it will move. Nothing will be impossible for you."*

And lo and behold, when I went back to pay the loan, my advisor told me that he had faith that I could achieve this goal and wanted to see it come to past for me. Since I had done so successfully, he was going to allow me to keep the loan money so that I could run a successful summer camp. This was a complete Hallelujah moment for me. My first real taste of faith to a prayer I was being hopeful for.To this Day, I remain humbled because of this experience.

I tell that story everywhere I go, because for me that is a classic example of having faith (no matter how little) and how being hopeful brings in doubts in your mind thereby eliminating whatever little faith you may have.

I jumped in to do a project that was way bigger than any other project I had ever done before and without the sufficient funds required for it to be successfully carried out.I could not have been more thankful to God for showing up and showing me the way at just the right time, and in this process I learned how to hold on to my faith.

This situation also taught me that the work that my not for profit organization is doing does not belong to me but instead to God, because through this organization I am caring for his children. And he will provide for his children just as he promised he would.

In **Matthew Chapter 19 - Verse 14**, where Jesus says, "*Let the little children come to me, and do not hinder them, for the kingdom of heaven belongs to such as these.*" And this is what made me to believe that if Jesus proclaimed that the Kingdom of Heaven does indeed belong to the little children, then he will surely provide a safe haven for them on Earth too.

Don't Forget God during the Storms and Sunshine

Often as humans, only when we are faced with rough times, do we become more hopeful in God and wish further that God will prevail. It is during those times that we must change our mindset from being hopeful to faithful in knowing that God is with us no matter if it is a good time or a bad time we are faced with. God will do what he said he would do.

In the book of **Mark, Chapter 11 – Verse 24**, Jesus says, *"Therefore I tell you, whatever you ask for in prayer, believe that you have received it, and it will be yours."* Through this verse, Jesus reminds us that we should continue to stay faithful no matter how hard the circumstances are or the situation we are stuck in. Hold on to your faith.

16

Our faith will help us get through some of the trials in life which seem unbearable. We must remind ourselves of the promises of God, and grab hold to the Holy Scriptures. Our faith will keep us in God's perfect peace.

I know this may seem easy to say, but harder to do; but it is true that our faith will help us speak things into existence even in the absence of an actual plan.

What is Hope? Why have Faith?

Coming back to the differentiation between Hope and Faith, Hope can be defined as an action which describes a person's thoughts focusing on uncertainty. It is when we essentially wish for an outcome which would work out to be conducive for us for the situation we are facing at that point in time.

While it is linked to faith, it is still considered to be associated with the fear of the unknown. Since we are unable to predict or foresee the future and what it holds for us, the outcome of a situation is equally unknown to us.

Thus, several of us are more hopeful that whatever the future holds, the outcome should result in our favor.

Faith on the other hand, unlike hope is based on the idea that whenever there is a good or bad situation in front of us, we let go and let God take control of whatever the outcome will be.

Faith enables us humans to put our trust and confidence in an unseen yet powerful being and we let go irrespective of the outcome of the situation. Faith requires us to be confident that no matter what the outcome, it is done so in our best interests.

While Faith is associated with the scriptures and religious doctrine to be precise, Hope is associated more with the logical reasoning of the human mind. Faith forces the believer to be completely reliant on the outcome of the decision rather than in the probability of what the outcome will be and as to how it will impact our life.

As I mentioned before, hope is logically inclined, it recognizes facts and simply wishes that the facts give out an outcome which is positive, whereas faith is based entirely on a blind resolution. When you have faith, you will believe that no matter what the facts are or the situation, the outcome you deserve will prevail for you in a given situation.

Faith does not approve or believe in the uncertainty unlike Hope. When you claim to have faith, you understand that the plan which has been decided by the Almighty is the only power which will make all things work in your favor and you have no choice but to accept it the way it is, irrespective of whether the outcome is positive or negative.

In my course and studies, I came across an article by Bishop T.D Jakes in the Charisma Magazine, which helped me furtherto understand what faith is and how we can prepare ourselves to let go and let God take over.

God wants your faith to be developed. Regardless of your position or your past, it is still faith that he will honor. God is in the business of restoring broken lives. If you believe that your background will keep you from moving forward with God, then you don't understand the value of faith.

Some people live good, clean, separated lives. Perhaps you are one of them. But if you want to grasp the things of God, you must understand that He will move in your life according to your faith, not according to your experience.

The main purpose of the scriptures is to imbibe in us the feeling of faith in God and His Son, Jesus and the faith to believe in his plan for us along with the faith to make the Word of God our way of life.

When we believe in the Word of God and do not have doubts about what is proclaimed, it is like planting a seed and providing it the required nourishment to watch it grow. In this case, when we plant the seed of faith in our heart and mind, we are willing to accept the plan as decided by God and the nourishment that we must use should be sourced from the Holy Bible which will enhance our faith in Our Father and his son Lord Jesus Christ.

If however, we only read the scriptures as an academic pursuit, we are not going to understand what actual faith is all about. Faith comes about when you are a witness to the Word of God, and as you continue to immerse yourself and practice as is preached in the scriptures, your faith will continue to mature and you will find yourself getting stronger in your belief that no matter what, you leave all the outcomes to God and trust in his will.

Be Strong in your Faith

Romans Chapter 10 – Verses 13 – 17 says, *"Everyone who calls on the name of the Lord will be saved. How, then, can they call on the one they have not believed in? And how can they believe in the one of whom they have not heard? And how can they hear without someone preaching to them? And how can anyone preach unless they are sent? As it is written: "How beautiful are the feet of those who bring good news!But not all the Israelites accepted the good news. For Isaiah says, "Lord, who has believed our message?" Consequently, faith comes from hearing the message, and the message is heard through the word about Christ."*

We can read the scriptures and allow the lives of others to serve as a means of strengthening our own faith.

Therefore, by immersing ourselves in the holy scriptures we not only attain wisdom through the power of the Holy Spirit but we also gain the faith that we possess so little of and the power of the spirit is how we can stand firm in our times of trials and tribulations.

Scriptures by themselves are considered to be a revelation, and by reading them and finding our way to living our lives through the scriptures, they will help in revealing much more to us if we put the Word of God to practice.

When we believe in something, we commit ourselves wholeheartedly to it. Because of the belief in us, we continue to strive and move forward irrespective of the hurdles that cross our paths.

As a Christian, faith is the focal point of our life. We profess during our service in Church that we have been saved because of our faith, and because of this we live by faith.

When you proclaim your faith, it means that you are telling the world that you believe in a statement or a claim made which stands true. Our faith reveals that we believe everything to be true which is mentioned in the scriptures about God, Jesus, and the Holy Spirit.

Our faith is what defines us as Christians and sets us apart from others who find the scriptures to be false or do not understand them the way we do. We see a split in several parts of the world amongst Christians, where some believe a part of the scripture while the others believe a second part, all according to their logic and not according to their faith. That, dear friend is not faith.

When we begin applying logic to the Word of God, we are beginning to let doubt and disbelief take over our mind and we then begin to question the statements mentioned in the scriptures.

When you claim that your faith is genuine, it means you trust God and his plan for you. When you say that you do indeed have faith, it will show in the little acts you do on a daily basis. If however, you do everything the opposite, i.e. not practice what has been preached in the scriptures, then your faith is only in your head and not in our heart.

And that faith is not really worth having if it is not helping you work on God's plan for you. Your faith should not push you only to believe in what is proclaimed in the Holy Scriptures about God, but it should push you to believe that there is a God and no matter where you are or what you do; he will always be with you, at your side, leading you along to what is meant for you.

When we do not have faith or trust in God, we are bound to become anxious and end up bringing on a host of illnesses upon ourselves. We begin to fear every outcome in any given situation we are confronted with and this leads to our own downfall.

When we learn to trust, our faith increases and we learn to rely entirely on God and his infinite mercy.

In today's world, we see so many of our own Christian brothers and sisters who are being made to leave their homes, the very homes they have grown up in and built their lives around. But they do not lose their faith; instead, they strive further and accept whatever comes their way since they know God is with them.

They do not let fear get to them since they believe in the Word of God, and if you have witnessed the Word of God, you will know that you will never be let down by it.

I'm sure we all have our own stories on how we built our faith. As I look back over my life I recognize that my life has been a faith walk. Many times I am not sure how something is going to be done, but I do have the faith to know that if I start the process than God will send what I need to complete it. You can look over your own life and reflect back on the many times God has been faithful to you. You were not sure on how the outcome will be, but it worked out for your good.

Yes God, I'm Listening!

Do Not Fear for the Lord is with You

Isaiah Chapter 43, Verse 1 – 5 proclaims, *"But now, this is what the Lord says—he who created you, Jacob, he who formed you, Israel: Do not fear, for I have redeemed you; I have summoned you by name; you are mine. When you pass through the waters, I will be with you; and when you pass through the rivers, they will not sweep over you. When you walk through the fire, you will not be burned; the flames will not set you ablaze. For I am the Lord your God, the Holy One of Israel, your Savior; I give Egypt for your ransom Cush[a] and Seba in your stead. Since you are precious and honored in my sight, and because I love you, I will give people in exchange for you, nations in exchange for your life. Do not be afraid, for I am with you*

Dr. Shanta Barton-Stubbs

I will bring your children from the east and gather you from the west."

While most of us want to work against evils such as war and violence which continues to build in different parts of the world, we need to respond to hatred and violence but not by using violence, instead as Christians in this world, we must make all efforts to use our faith and the Word of God in explaining to others who do not believe and strengthen their faith in God almighty too.

Let go of fear by trusting God with your life and for whatever the future holds for you. Do not fear, believe and you will find yourself passing through life's hurdles unharmed and safe.

Because at the end of the day, faith alone can help you overcome your fear, be it a personal fear or whether the fear is generational or globally.

Let us take the example of David. He was betrayed by his own son before the enemies surrounded him, driving him into exile, despite being threatened by his enemies, David boldly says, *"Whom shall I fear? Of whom shall I be afraid?"* David knew his faith was the strongest point for him to overcome his fear of death.

In the letter of Paul to the Romans, he states, *"If God is for us, who is against us?"* He further writes, *"Who will separate us from the love of Christ? Will hardship, or distress, or persecution, or famine, or nakedness, or peril or sword? No, in all these things we are more than conquerors through him who loved us. For I am convinced that neither death nor life, nor angels, nor rulers, nor things present, nor things to come, nor powers, nor height, nor depth, nor anything else in all creation, will be able to separate us from the love of God in Christ Jesus our Lord."* Thereby proving that his faith was his

31

secret to overcoming the fear while he was imprisoned. His wholehearted belief in the Word of God and in his Holy Son Lord Jesus Christ gave him more power to rejuvenate his faith in the Lord and trust in him completely.

God is going to take care of you!

Rev. Martin Luther King, whom I fondly remember for his beautiful and meaningful stories,narrated a story on overcoming fear irrespective of what they all feared.

This story I have shared below is an essay titled 'Strength to Love' from his book, 'A Testament of Hope: The Essential Writings and Speeches of Martin Luther King, Jr.To live amongst a community threatened with harm to their lives, knowing that they had extremely high chances of losing their lives, they carried on with their daily duties including preaching the Word of God to their fellow community members.

Martin Luther King, irrespective of what he was and what he is remembered for will mostly be recalled as a person who found his courage in trusting God and letting him take over the reign of his life. Below I share the

33

story as narrated by Rev. King which till this date makes me proud to share it with you too.

"One of the most dedicated participants in the bus protest in Montgomery, Alabama," he writes, *"was an elderly Negro whom we affectionately called 'Mother Pollard.' Although poverty-stricken and uneducated, she was amazingly intelligent and possessed a deep understanding of the meaning of the movement. After having walked for several weeks, she was asked if she were tired. With ungrammatical profundity, she answered, 'My feet are tired, but my soul is rested.'*

"On a particular Monday evening," Dr. King continues, *"following a tension-packed week which included being arrested and receiving numerous threatening phone calls, I spoke at a mass meeting. I attempted to convey an overt impression of strength and*

Yes God, I'm Listening!

courage, although I was inwardly depressed and fear-stricken.

At the end of the meeting, Mother Pollard came to the front of the church and said, 'Come here, son.' I immediately went to her and hugged her affectionately. 'Something is wrong with you,' she said. 'You didn't talk strong tonight.' Seeking further to disguise my fears, I retorted, 'Oh, no, Mother Pollard, nothing is wrong. I am feeling as fine as ever.' 'Now you can't fool me,' she said. 'I know something is wrong. Is it that we ain't doing things to please you? Or is it that the white folks are bothering you?' Before I could respond, she looked directly into my eyes and said, 'I don told you we is with you all the way.'

Then, her face became radiant and she said in quiet certainty, 'But even if we aren't with you, God's going take care of you.' As she spoke these consoling words," says King, "everything in me quivered and quickened with the tremor of raw energy.

"Since that dreary night in 1956," he goes on to say in his story, "Mother Pollard has passed on to glory and I have known very few quiet days. I have been tortured without and tormented within by the raging fires of tribulation. I have been forced to muster what strength and courage I have to withstand howling winds of pain and jostling storms of adversity. But as the years have unfolded the eloquently simple words of Mother Pollard have come back again and again to give light and peace and guidance to my troubled soul. 'God is going take care of you.'

The real meaning of faith is when you realize the value of giving more than receiving in your life. It is when you begin to understand and share the life transforming relationship with the one you put your complete faith in –

God. When you 'walk with God', you indicate that you share a relationship which reflects one of love, fidelity and trust.

It does not matter if you give your assent to claims made about God, but by allowing yourself to be led by the way God intended for you, and by doing so, you are also enriching your experience with God Almighty as well as reaching out to others by showcasing your relationship with God.

While writing this chapter, I have quoted several verses from the scriptures, at the same time I have also stressed on how vital our relationship with God is and it can only be a successful relationship when we begin to accept God's way in our lives.

When we believe in the love of God and his Son Jesus, we should also understand that we will not be spared from the regular experiences of human life. When I say this, I mean, just because I talk of faith in God, you should not expect life to be perfect. I do not say that just by having faith and being strong in your belief in God you will not have any pain to deal with.

If you are putting your faith in God only so that you can have a perfect life, then my friend, your faith is not in your heart, but more in your mind, and as harsh as it may sound, having faith which makes you see logic in everything that comes your way is not worth your walk with God.

Faith in God does not mean we are exempted from trials and tribulations in our human life, instead having faith in God changes us in how we deal with the trials which come our way. Faith changes the way we respond to uncomfortable situations in our life. It teaches us to be stronger when we are faced with fear.

When we feel our faith, we know that in the deepest part of our heart, that all will be well despite things seeming like they are going downhill for us. Our faith becomes our silent assurance which comforts and calms us even though we may not be feeling at the top of the world. Faith provides us with the power we need to face the realities of our day to day lives, to accept that while things may not be perfect, you will be blessed with what is meant for you.

We cannot produce or manufacture faith, it often comes to us during our difficult times and rather unexpected. Once we experience faith, it will help us to recall over and over again our true relationship with God.

Our faith and hope can't be in our material possessions. This world is judged on things that people have and wish they had. Be grateful not to be one of those people who are stuck on things which can easily be lost or replaced.

Materialistic items are the root of a lot of issues in this world today. People are always trying to follow the trends and get items that they see the rich and famous with. I don't have faith for the hope of materialistic things but something with way more substance.

I'm not sure why so many people rely on certain things to become successful in life. Materialistic things are a lot of those things that people want to ask for. If you seek God, and do his will, things will come.

Even I have issues with my faith from time to time. My faith is mostly tested when I feel I am in desperate need for the youth center that I provide services for. There are times when I feel that people may not support or times when I feel that God may not provide, but I'm quickly reminded of God's promises.

God has given me this mission not for me to worry but for me to know that he will provide. I am always so grateful to see people extend blessings towards the mission so that we may continue to strive.

This organization has helped me grow in so many areas not only physically but spiritually as well. My faith has been increased by seeing God do it over and over again.

Do Not Be Discouraged

There was one particular time when it was Christmas and I didn't have much for the kids at New Image. Bills were behind at the facility, times were getting tough and the work hours that I had were very little. I wasn't sure how we were going to take care of the bills which we had and I began to become very discouraged.

My father reminded me of God's grace and how he will provide although I did not see a way. I have to admit I had a hard time believing and knowing that it was going to be okay, my father requested that I give it one week of prayer and fasting to see what God would do.

Although I was very discouraged although I was aware of God's miracles and had experienced them before and decided to give it one week before giving up. During that one week, I did pray and I did fast and negative thoughts that came my way were destroyed by repeating the word of God and believing in the faith which I yet still had.

To be honest with you, I think my faith was probably the size of a mustard seed, but I did have something to hold onto. (Once again, I had just the right amount of faith to hold on to) I walked into Walmart not even knowing exactly what was going to take place to purchase some items were my sister was working at that time.

My sister passed along the phone number of a guy she met while ringing up his transactions.

As he was coming down her lane she began to ring up his items and noticed that he had a lot of toys and she begin to talk to him about his church and his outreach ministries.

She began to tell my story of the New Image Youth Center on how I got started and how hard it was for me to keep things up on my own for over 20 students at the time on an everyday basis. This same guy ended up being a pastor for a church and began to share with my sister how he would like to help and jump on board for Christmas for the students that I served.

I quickly called and this church was a blessing to my organization. They did not know me only from what I shared and the information my sister shared. The Church provided a Christmas gift for every one of my youth including bicycles and other items and even financial donations.

All of this occurred in the seven days that my dad told me to fast, pray and believe God. I still look back on that situation and just receive a feeling of gratefulness of knowing how God did not leave us out. That was amazing how he used my sister as an instrument to speak up and my sister normally fights with the thought of thinking that she does not have a true purpose in life.

I often remind her of the situation, and how God used her for the youth that I serve.

It's the stories like this that keeps my faith strong and gives me the understanding of knowing that my faith is not based on materialistic things but things that are bigger than I.

When my faith is low it's only because I have not been in the word of God the way I should, or I have allowed other things to distract me at the moment. When I am reminded of the goodness of God my faith is restored and begins to come alive in me.

If we truly believe that God's word will do what it says it will do then we should have no problem having faith to believe that God can do what we feel may be the impossible. Actually there is no impossibilities with God, all things are possible as we are reminded in the Scriptures

In the Bible, **Mark, Chapter 9, Verse 23** states, *"...If you can?" said Jesus. "Everything is possible for one who believes."*

Doubts in your Faith

I can understand as a baby Christian how sometimes we may have doubts and not be quite sure of the things that God can do, but as mature Christians it's hard for me to understand why we doubt God and sometimes do not put our faith into action.

I'm speaking from a personal stance and know that I have known God for a very long time and have seen him do some miraculous things. Even in this, at times I'll doubt his word and doubt that he will come through although he manages to put my doubt aside and show me that his word cannot and will not lie.

I'm here writing and thinking of what would make me doubt God. A God who has been there for me and so many others so very often and has proven himself over and over again. I am the one who often falls short of

47

his word, but yet he shows himself to me over and over again.

There are times when I just sit and wonder what is wrong with all of us. In fact, what is wrong with me that despite being blessed with so many things all my life, I continue to have moments where I still doubt all the goodness God has provided me in my life. I still continue to doubt his work, despite having seen the results reflect in my everyday life.

There is a term we often use in the mental health field coined "adjustment". Readjustments take place when someone who has experienced a change in their life which has affected their work, their school, their ability to think in normal dynamics, and has caused them to have to change some things in order to focus clearly. I understand and recognize this especially when change happens unexpectedly; it takes a minute to adjust to the new surroundings and the new issue accordingly.

As Children of God, often at a young age where the mind is still in formation, I observe and sense adjusting to the new lifestyle and having those moments where you do feel anxious not knowing if God is going to answer your prayer; but as mature Christians I find it very hard to understand why is it so hard for us to adjust to the fact that God's word cannot lie and will do exactly what he said he would do.

There's no other explanation to this, but to know that once you pray, God will hear it and fulfill it according to his will.

Making your Faith Stronger

You can help make your faith stronger by following some of the ways below. These are all based from my observation of what I have done and this has surely helped me to build my faith and make my walk with God more fruitful and beneficial to me spiritually as well.

1. **Practice Recall** – By practicing recall, you will be able to remember all the times when God has been good to you and blessed you with things you need or pulled you out of a troublesome situation even when you have not turned to God for the same.

   But you should also recall the good times God has blessed you with. When you recall all the good and bad memories, you will find the strength to stay strong when you are facing a hard time.

2. **Detach Yourself** – When you believe that God is at work and has a plan for you, you need to let go of specific ideas of how you want your life to be. By detaching yourself, you will find yourself with the freedom to work out things which will bring you contentment and peace of mind.

    Trust God in every situation and reach out to him when you feel like you are low on faith in any given circumstance. Trust in him to bring you out victorious even though you feel like you have been defeated.

3. **Be Grateful** – No matter what the circumstances are, be thankful for what you have. Don't be thankful only

for the good things in your life, but for the pain and the suffering as well.

Let's admit it, only when you are faced with the trials and tribulations is when you will be able to accept your relationship with God and work on improving it as well. And I think that sure does need thanks.

Get into the habit of being grateful for the people in your life or the job you have. Practice being grateful instead of being morose and complaining or comparing yourself to what others have.

When you do so you will realize that you do have the best and all that you require in your life.

4. **Be Good, Do Good**—Your faith will increase when we share it with others who are a part of our life. You will find that love deepens further when you are able to share it with others.

When I talk about love, I don't mean only love that you feel for your near and dear ones. When I say love, I mean the feeling you get when you serve others who are in need.

That joy of being able to serve those who are in dire need of help. It need not be monetary help, but it could be by utilizing your time in serving others such as the elderly or any orphanage where there are so many children who are given up.

Volunteer for any cause which you are comfortable with. It could also be at a pet shelter or rescue work during stormy times. Use the many talents you have been blessed with by serving those who have no easy way of learning or are unable to afford a class.

As **John, Chapter 12, Verse 26** states, *"Whoever serves me must follow me; and where I am, my servant also will be. My Father will honor the one who serves me."*

5. **Increase your Trust** —As **Psalm 56, Verse 3** states in the scriptures, *"When I am afraid, I will put my trust in You."* Whenever you are facing a moment of doubt, where you feel that fear is getting to you, close your eyes and remember the Lord.

Take a deep breath and in your mind pray to God. Ask him to watch over

Yes God, I'm Listening!

you. Believe that he is there by your side come rain or sunshine. A prayer is nothing but your way of communicating with God.

Surrender everything unto him, all your worries, all your thoughts. It won't be long before you find yourself calmer and in a much better position to confront whatever awaits you and what you are afraid of.

1 Peter Chapter 5, Verse 7 says, *"Cast all your anxiety on him because he cares for you."* Your prayer does not have to be too long, even a short prayer can work miracles. All you need to do is put your trust in Him!

As humans, we cannot escape fear, raising doubts in our minds or even suffering. However, if we just let go and believe in the love of God and his mercy, we will realize that things could have been far worse from what they are,and it is not really all that bad.

The gift of faith can be the best gift of all if you realize how valuable it is and the impact it has on your life.

When you believe with your heart, mind and your entire soul, your life will surely turn around and give you the confidence to take any task you find difficult head on with no cares or worries to bog you down. This is when you know that your faith has taken over.

Chapter 2: Watch that Tongue!

In this chapter, I talk about how the most powerful weapon on this planet; your tongue can make or break you. We often forget what we say and before even thinking it through, we usually blurt it all out unknowing to the pain and damage it might have caused.

The tongue can cause severe devastation and even then I think devastation would be an understatement to use especially since I have seen families being torn apart because of some nasty things said to one another.

As people of God, we must learn to heed to the advice as shared with us in the Holy Scriptures.

The Tongue and its Powers

The tongue can build up, encourage, and inspire, or it can bring about miracles and healing to oneself. The same very important device can tear down and bring about destruction in families, in the home, in the workplace, and in the church.

It can cause strife, pain, hardship and many other negative attributes. The tongue can equally bring about blessings, and curses. With our tongues, we can usher in a spirit of worship, praise, and open the floodgates of heaven.

We can also tear down strongholds, send back demonic forces, and plead the blood of Jesus. With this same device, we can also bring about oppression, sickness and disease of the mind, body, and soul.

This is the reason, whenever you are angry, you are advised to 'watch your tongue', because once words are spoken, there is really no way you can take them back and no amount of apologizing will help you mend your relationship with the person you have been verbally harsh with.

In the process of understanding the importance of the tongue, you have to be more conscious of the statements which you allow yourself to put out in any given situation because those very statements can determine your life.

While it does sound like a simple concept, but yet we allow ourselves to say what we want freely thinking there's no validity to our words. Our words can be responsible for some of our current situations, good or bad equally.

There have been plenty of times in my life where I have made statements in public without realizing how it will impact my own life, but as humans, for us speaking without thinking has become a part of the norm and that is something we must strive to control.

Whenever you feel like you are going to begin with a barrage of words especially those spoken in anger, you must find a way to calm yourself and correct your words before you speak them lest you end up destroying and losing a relationship which is valuable to you.

Similarly, in our relationship with God, we tend to lose our thoughts when we are faced with troubles. We often tend to forget the fact that God has shown us some good days and hence there are bound to be a few bad days.

Given our mindset, we always want the good and are never prepared for the worst. So when we are faced with some troublesome times, our first reaction is to always curse our fate and at times even abuse God.

I am sure there are several of us who have been through such situations, only to regret what we have said when we realize the bad day actually was good since we got something better than what we actually deserved.

Ephesians Chapter 4, Verse 29 states, *"Do not let any unwholesome talk come out of your mouths, but only what is helpful for building others up according to their needs, that it may benefit those who listen."*

The tongue can create scars which are never easy to heal, and this powerful weapon is used by people of all ages, castes, religions. Even in The Holy Bible, we read about how the tongue has great power, to destroy or heal, to spread love or to spew hatred against your fellow beings.

Most of us don't even recognize the words we speak become our life. How motivating and scary this could be at the same time, depending on the words we choose to say.

The day I did became aware of how important my words were; I chose to become more careful with what I said and how I conveyed it to the concerned person. However, there are still times I would speak ill minded or speak things into existence which I did not want to take place.

Once I became more aware of this, I would quickly retract the negativity and ask God to forgive me for being ignorant or speaking ignorant since I know the word. Ignorant to the extent that I would not want those things to become my reality although I spoke them so freely.

However, asking God for forgiveness when you make a mistake does not mean you can say anything and everything to people and then apologize to God. It doesn't work that way.

Being aware about what you say and how you say it is an everyday learning process although I am very aware of my words, I still yet continue to make mistakes while making statements which are not edifying to the life I live or the life I represent at times or the life I intend to produce.

However, now, I do make it my business to be more proactive by being in control of the things that I say and being sure to be an example of Christ; I now speak of things which are empowering, motivating and edifying and depict behavior as should be carried out as stated in the scriptures.

In my line of work it is very easy to empower, to motivate, to encourage others, however, there have been times when I am low, overworked and do not really represent a person who has everything sorted or balanced out.

During this time, I may begin to speak things which I know could be corrupting although I may not be completely in a healthy mental place. When I recognize that God is not doing the things that I would like him to do when I want him to, then I may also become guilty of sometimes speaking corruption.

Learning to be more in control of my own personal statements is something that I have recognized I need to apply more in detail in every area of my life. Just as I can encourage and inspire others I need to also inspire myself to change those areas which need to be corrected.

Currently, I am moving forward and I am progressing towards turning into a better me and in order to do that it will take practice and all the effort I can muster up, but it will also take the willingness and acceptance to commit to my wrongdoing and becoming more aware of the areas that I am weak in.

I have noticed that I have spoken things into existence or I have said things out of malice, hatred or even deceit. I have never admitted to being perfect, but I am willing to strive towards perfection. So, I can see now that when I speak ill, most likely I'm not in the word of God the way I should be.

The word of God should help me become more open and able to control my confessions and the statements which come out of my mouth. I need to constantly renew my mind with the word of God. I'm learning to guard my heart, my mouth, and my eyes by staying in tune with the word of God.

Human Speech and the Tongue

The way a person speaks can reveal quite a lot about his character. Even in the scriptures, Jesus Christ warns his disciples as well as his followers at his gatherings with regard to certain kind of language being used that comes from a person's mouth.

We even notice this being warned by God in the Ten Commandments which signify a person's speech. One of the commandments warns against taking the name of the Lord God in vain wherein the other commandment, God heeds us to not bear false witness against any other person.

We also read about Jesus' Sermon on the Mount where he warns those present, as quoted from **Matthew Chapter 5, Verses 33-37**, "Again, you have heard that it was said to the people long ago, *"Do not break your oath, but fulfill to the Lord the oaths you have made. But I tell you, do not swear an oath at all: either by heaven, for it is God's throne; or by the earth, for it is his footstool; or by Jerusalem, for it is the city of the Great King. And do not swear by your head, for you cannot make even one hair*

Yes God, I'm Listening!
white or black. All you need to say is simply
"Yes," or "No"; anything beyond this comes
from the evil one."

In the scriptures, when we read them and
study them properly, you will find different
kinds of speech mentioned.

As I had mentioned before as humans we are
prone to speaking whatever comes to our
mind when angry. One of the tongues which
is most spoken of in The Bible is the hateful
tongue. In the scriptures, Jeremiah speaks of
people who are treacherous and bend their
tongue like bows.

He cautions us through the scriptures that
one should not believe in people who deceive
others through slander nor should we
interact with those who have taught how to
only lie. We have been blessed with a tongue
but instead of doing well or saying well, we
often choose to just rip somebody apart by
passing nasty comments about them.

The boasting tongue is another tongue which is widely spoken about in The Bible. The Pharisee in the Bible is boastful before the Lord.

There is a popular saying about "a bragging man being preferred only by the fools but looked down upon by the wise." We come across so many people in our lives on a daily basis who cannot carry forward a conversation with you because all they can do is boast about their accomplishments and self adulation.

While we may tolerate it by being courteous and listening to their stories, it does not bode well with God.

Many of us are guilty of the boastful tongue. Saying things, to try to prove a false point to others has become the new norm in this day and time. It is fine for us to be successful, and to want to celebrate with others, but it's another thing to boast to make yourself appear to be more than who you really are. A boastful tongue is one who speaks out of content, in order to seek attention or acceptance from a person or a group of people.

Dr. Shanta Barton-Stubbs

The Pharisee and the Tax Collector

In **Luke Chapter 18, verses 9 – 14**, we read about the parable of the Pharisee and the tax collector.

To some who were confident of their own righteousness and looked down on everyone else, Jesus told this parable: *"Two men went up to the temple to pray, one a Pharisee and the other a tax collector. The Pharisee stood by himself and prayed: 'God, I thank you that I am not like other people—robbers, evildoers, adulterers—or even like this tax collector. I fast twice a week and give a tenth of all I get.*

But the tax collector stood at a distance. He would not even look up to heaven, but beat his breast and said, 'God, have mercy on me, a sinner. I tell you that this man, rather than the other, went home justified before God.

70

For all those who exalt themselves, they will be humbled, and those who humble themselves will be exalted."

In today's day and age I do not think there is even one of us who hasn't criticized anyone, whether it is a famous actor or actress about a role they played in the latest Hollywood flick or whether it is a colleague at work, or somebody you know at Church.

We tend to criticize a lot sometimes and often it becomes such a bad habit that whenever we run out of conversational topics, we end up finding reasons to criticize more people and it can get so worse where it can lead to us hating a person for no fault of theirs at all.

While you may argue and say that constructive criticism is helpful and works well for some people especially those belonging to the creative fields, we should be able to set a boundary when it comes to constructive criticism.

Any wise person will understand the criticism given to his or her work and use it wisely to his benefit, however, I have come across several people who have turned criticism into a hobby of sorts which I feel is just being mean! **Proverbs Chapter 17, Verse 10** says, *"A rebuke is more effective with a man of understanding than a hundred lashes to a fool."*

I am sure most of you have come across people in your lives who speak the double tongue. Before I go any further, let me explain who a double tongue speaking person is.

Have you ever come across a person who says things to you only so that he or she can fill your ears, and then go to a second person and say something entirely different to another person.

This kind of person is an ace at playing a double face because his tongue says one thing and then he does something entirely different. You can never trust such a person or take their word for anything.

Proverbs Chapter 8, Verse 8 says, *"All the utterances of my mouth are in righteousness; there is nothing crooked or perverted in them."*

To conclude this chapter, I would like to quote **Ephesians Chapter 4, Verse 29**, *"Let no corrupting talk come out of your mouths, but only such as is good for building up, as fits the occasion, that it may give grace to those who hear."*

As humans, I believe we bear some responsibility towards how we take care of our relationship with others who are a part of our lives like our family and friends and those who we continue to meet in life. What we say to them does matter. How we speak about them determines who we really are. Our words are important and we should be more aware of the words which we allow to escape our mouths.

As the scriptures state, we must absolutely try to keep our tongues in check when we speak.

Don't let your mind rule over your tongue and when you do learn to control your thoughts, you will be able to watch your tongue and be more cautious while speaking. If speaking in anger to someone watch your words. If you find yourself getting extremely opinionated while providing someone with constructive criticism, check yourself, and watch that tongue.

Chapter 3: Renew your Mind, Renew your Faith!

It's amazing to know the moment we speak and say the sinner's prayer and ask for forgiveness we are instantly born of the Spirit of God. It always humbles me to know that God's requirement for being called his child does not require a whole lot like we would think.

We must confess with our mouth we are sinners, believe in our hearts that Jesus died on the cross and rose again on the third day so that we may have life and have it for eternity, accordingly to **Romans Chapter 10, Verse 9**.

And after accepting Christ into our hearts then it's time for the work to begin which includes being able to transform and change ourselves by the renewing of our minds through the word of God.

Renewing of our minds does not sound like a hard process, but this can be a battle if not done correctly by using the word of God. We all have our certain ways of thinking, but the moment we become children of Christ we must begin to think the way he will want us to think and eliminate all the negativity and reject the enemies thought pattern.

Any thought that is not of Christ,and any way of thinking which will cause a distraction, any ill feelings towards others, all details negative or erroneous thinking. As a humanistic being, it is easy for us to come up with our own way of thinking, but renewing our minds requires time with God and reading his word.

The more we are engaged in his word the more we are open for change. There is no way to be effective with an unstable mindset. We can't have both a mindset of Christ and of the world at the same time and expect to be stable.

Having the Mindset of Christ

In the scriptures, **James, Chapter 1, Verse 8** it says, *"...Such a person is double-minded and unstable in all they do."*

In order to be stable, one MUST have the mind of Christ.

I have experienced this many times before in my own personal life where I have noticed a change when I have not been able to spend time with God. I find myself thinking and even saying things that I normally would not say. It flows so effortlessly out of my mouth when not keyed in with the Spirit of God, but when I am in my word, I am more aware and in control of the things that I think and say.

Even before I begin to say something negative my spirit man begins to warn me and stop me in advance.I know what it feels like to be double minded and the chaos it brings.

There is no peace in that life and in order to succeed in any area of life one must have the mind of Christ. I believe in this more than I can even share. With the mind of Christ, I know that all things are possible and will work together for my good.

Romans Chapter 8, Verse 28 says, *"And we know that God causes all things to work together for good to those who love God, to those who are called according to His purpose."*

It's the enemy's job to prevent us from being our best and trying to inject us with negativity but with the Spirit of God the Spirit can always override the enemy's negative intent as long as we are doing our part by staying prayerful and being in the word of God.

At the end of the day, it's God's ultimate desire to completely take charge of our spirit, soul and body. This allows us to understand that our spirit shall be one of Christ, allowing him to intervene in us.

Our soul shall be one that represents the Spirit of God and everything that we say and do with our body should also be under subjection and willing to line up with the word of God.

The more I renew my mind, my body, and my soul will begin to line up with the word of God and reflect the life of Christ.

I often think about how certain things come a part of you because they have entered you in some way, things such as sickness, disease, jealousy, hatred, being unforgiving and other negative characteristics.

These ungodly characteristics and spirits can easily enter into my spirit man just by me allowing my mindset to be on other things which are not of God. We often ask God why certain things happen to us not even recognizing that certain things we are causing to happen to ourselves.

Checking our mindset should be a daily process of evaluating and analyzing what we are thinking, and what we are allowing to enter into our spirit. Our mind appears to be the key to our walk with God. If we can maintain the mindset of Christ then we can conquer all things using his word.

It is God's ultimate intent to be in full control of our life if we allow him to. I have often recognized that things have entered my mind and my body because I have not remained in the word of God in prayer the way that I should.

By keeping the mind of Christ I must not allow my spirit to be open to anything. When I become aware of certain things not representing Christ being around me I must exit the situation in order to guard my own spirit man. I use to think that I was strong enough to encounter these situations, but why even allow my spirit to be grieved with such negativity.

 The enemy will try to put flashbacks in my mind to keep me from moving forward but as long as I maintain the Spirit of God and continue to do his will then my mind will be set on those things which are ahead not behind me.

There are times when the enemy will have someone to use my past as a way to ridicule me, embarrass me, or try to attack my character but once I recognize this behavior I am able to address it and remind the enemy that I am not that and I am strong enough through the help of Christ.

Yes God, I'm Listening!

People indication of me doesn't define me as long as I have moved forward and God has forgiven me. Maintaining the mind of Christ does take work but requires me to humble myself and be subjective and open to hearing what God wants to say to me.

Just like a new week beginning on a Monday gives us the opportunity to start anew, our walk with Jesus Christ and his father gives us that same new opportunity in discovering ourselves and his plan for us.

Romans Chapter 12, Verse 2 states, *"Don't copy the behavior and customs of this world, but let God transform you into a new person by changing the way you think. Then you will learn to know God's will for you, who is good and pleasing and perfect."*

When we put our mind to getting a particular task done, our attitude towards how that task should be done changes.

In the Bible, Paul tells us that if we change the way we look at how things are done, we are bound to change the way we think about it. Changing our mindset can not only help us in achieving what we have set out to conquer but can also help us transform our lives.

The Bible encourages us time and again about choosing a mindset which befits our walk with God. We should understand what our priorities are in this walk with God and how we should focus solely on those priorities.

Yes God, I'm Listening!

Turn to the Lord

When you feel like everything is going wrong and you are unable to process why, put your focus on God's word found in the scriptures and you will be able to confront life's challenges.

As a Christian and a believer in God, there are times I am absolutely distraught about how I have spent previous years fretting over anything and everything. Sure, I did go to Church, but most of time was spent being disappointed about the people walking out of my life and about the things I could not achieve, I had absolutely no peace since I was always guilty and condemning my behavior.

However, once I decided that all I needed to do was change my way of thinking about my successes and failures, I seemed to have had a wonderful transformation. I begun trusting

85

in The Lord and I'm ensured that it stuck on as a habit.

Now, when I look back, while I do feel bad for having wasted some time doing nothing which was Christ like in behavior, but at the same time I am thankful for letting God letting me go through that phase since it is the only way I discovered Gods will for my life and have since gotten closer to him.

The Word of God calls upon us to have confidence in God and through the scriptures we hear him and his Word. Just like our meals are consumed on a daily basis, the Bible is our spiritual food and should be consumed daily as well.

When we are feeling down and low, we should attempt to spend time reading the scriptures and then meditating on it so that we are able to understand what is it exactly that the Word of God is teaching us.

There have been numerous occasions where I haven't been in the best of moods, and somehow I have managed to open up a page from The Bible with a verse which related to the situation I have been placed in.

When you begin meditating upon the scriptures you read, you begin to feel the Word of God having its impact in your life.

When you let go of your own thoughts, you begin to experience the word of God and begin to trust him wholehearted; it is indeed a joyous experience when you understand what your role is on this planet and what it is that God has actually intended for you to do.

Chapter 4: Positive Affirmation for Change

I do believe the phrase that we are what we think and what we speak. Therefore I will control my tongue by only stating those things which are conducive to the lifestyle which I am reaching for. In order for me to maintain this lifestyle I must change my mindset and the way that I think about life in general.

My mouth would affirm positive statements and in return those positive statements will become my reality. I am not only changing my mindset in the way that I think but I am also changing the words which I allow to come from my mouth.

Daily Verbal Affirmations

Affirmations strengthen us by helping us believe in the potential of what we desire to manifest in our own life. When we verbally affirm our thoughts and ambitions we are empowered and know that they can come to past. Read these affirmations out loud:

I am superior to negative thoughts and low actions.

I have been giving the tools which I begin to utilize today.

I forgive those who have harmed me and my past and peacefully detach from them now.

I possess everything which is needed in order to be extremely successful.

My life represents the life of Christ and I am overflowing in blessings and

Miracles.

I have more than enough and I am able to bless others.

My potential to succeed is infinite.

Life is just beginning and I am in control of my thoughts, my feelings, and my expressions.

I am able to find solutions to challenges and Roadblocks which will happen in my life and I am able to move past them quickly.

I am successful today I will be even more successful tomorrow and even the more the next day.

God has equipped me with the power that I need on a daily basis to fight against the wiles of the enemy.

The anointing on my life makes the difference and will show in everything that I do as long as I apply it every day. Miracles signs and wonders are all around me and I decree that they take place in my life in all that I do.

God has left an inheritance for me that I may enjoy the fruits of the land and shall not go without.

I shall call in and decree the things which I want to see in my life daily and affirm that they will take place just as I say them because I have the power to call things into existence.

Chapter 5: The Anointing of God

The anointing makes the difference. It seems to be simple logical science, but yet it is so hard for us to grasp the fact that the anointing is way more powerful than most of us can even wrap our understanding around.

As people, I think we have become complacent to saying everyday clichés such as the anointing makes the difference or it's been the anointing on my life but yet we do not practice our beliefs.

The anointing can take us to our full potential. The anointing is something that cannot be replaced and cannot be denied. The anointing of God is something that would change the entire atmosphere when it comes around.

Yes God, I'm Listening!

I'm sure we have all experienced the anointing of God but yet many of us have yet to experience it to its ultimate magnitude. Why are we so afraid to experience God in that manner?

The anointing in our life can open doors which have been closed. The anointing in our lives can be used to bring others to Christ which is our ultimate job once we become born again.

The word of God shares that once we are anointed it remains with us. In **1 John Chapter 2, Verse 27** the words says, "*But the anointing which ye have received of him abide in you, and ye need not that any man teach you: but as the same anointing teaches you of all things, and is truth, and is no lie, and even as it hath taught you, ye shall abide in him.*"

The anointing of God will be our teacher and will lead us, but yet so many of us are looking for something to fulfill us, and it's been here the entire time, the Anointing of God.

The anointing of God is not something that comes on us and leaves on a regular basis but instead we are the one who walks into the anointing and then leave it. I doubt that we even know the true meaning of what the anointing stands for in our lives or what it can do for our lives.

The anointing of God it's not temporary but something that was meant to stay; however we often abandon it and attempt to pick up it when we are in need. I can only imagine or should I say I am about to experience what life is like walking in the anointed of God. I have to admit that I haven't received the anointing in its fullest capacity, because I have set limits and restraints on what the anointing can do in my life.

It's amazing to see and hear the stories of God's anointing. The bible states in **Luke**

Chapter 4, Verse 18, *"The Spirit of the Lord [is] upon me, because he hath anointed me to preach the gospel to the poor; he hath sent me to heal the brokenhearted, to preach deliverance to the captives, and recovering of sight to the blind, to set at liberty them that are bruised."*

This is the work of the ones who are anointed. I can't say that my resume looks this good. I do know that I am anointed to do God's will, but after being reminded of the signs and wonders which should follow me, I know that I must begin to seek God more in order to work in the lives of the people, heal the sick, open blind eyes, and heal the broken hearted, etc.

It's amazing to experience God and apply the word to your life properly. God's anointing is something that cannot be duplicated or replaced by any other spiritual being. The anointing definitely makes the difference if it is applied in your life as the word leads us to do.

Operating an after school/summer camp non-profit organization I have found that many times mentally and physically I began to get tired and worried if God will provide.

I believe that God is going to provide but yet when I see things getting pretty slim, or becoming difficult, I begin to doubt what's going to take place and if God will show up. It's not until my spirit man began to remind me about the anointing on my life, that I can decree it and see it happen before me.

In the word of God, I become strengthened and reminded that my God will meet all my needs according to the riches of his glory in Christ Jesus accordingly to **Philippians Chapter 4, Verse 19** which states, *"And my God will supply every need of yours according to his riches in glory in Christ Jesus."*

Yes God, I'm Listening!

God has been very faithful to me over the last 12 years with New Image Youth Center. Out of the twelve years, I have seen many people start something, but yet not finish. People often ask me how am I able to stay so dedicated to the organization and my simple answer is I am anointed for this work.

Unfortunately many people begin to start something and stop. They just stop it when they get tired or when they feel things are getting hard for them to deal with.

This is the same thing many people do with the anointing of God. We forget that that we have the power and are anointed to do all things through Christ which strengthens us.

If you read the scriptures, you will find reference of this in **Philippians Chapter 4, Verse 13** which states, *"And my God will supply all your needs according to His riches in glory in Christ Jesus."*

Although there are times when we may not feel anointed, or we don't see the anointing working in its full potential in our lives doesn't mean that it no longer exists.

That's the time we should begin to activate the anointed in us, by praying, fasting, and reading the word of God. We must continue to cultivate that anointing that is amongst us, and which abides in us.

When troubles come you should not worry, stress, or even doubt God. Give it to God, all of yourissues; because with the anointing of God you know that it's already worked out.

Unfortunately, most of us do the total opposite with our father. We doubt, pout and make excuses when things don't go right, instead of using the word of God which reminds us that we have the anointing to make mountains move. Say to that mountain, you must move because the anointing in me demands it today.

Yes God, I'm Listening!

I have learned to walk in the anointing of God now more than ever. I can see when I am walking in the anointing of God and when I'm not.

When I am walking in the anointing of God things appear to work out for my good. Things fall into place when I walk in Gods anointing, and when I do not walk in his anointing I feel naked. I feel alone, I feel unjust, and I feel unproductive.

I am not sure what it would take for me to understand that I have the ability to walk in God's anointing every day and sometimes I choose not to. Why? I don't know when I can clearly see that walking in his anointing brings joy, love, peace, understanding and other fruits of the spirit.

Galatians Chapter 5, Verses 22-23 state, *"But the fruit of the Spirit is love, joy, peace, patience, kindness, goodness, faithfulness,* *gentleness, self-control; against such things there is no law...."*

I feel that with God's anointing I can have anything, I can do anything, I can conquer everything. Without it, it's totally opposite. After being reminded of God's anointing, I will be crazy not to apply this to my life everyday. Why don't we as believers?

I need God's anointing more than I can even say. His anointing is almost like the breath in my body; it's that one thing that you know is for sure and cannot change.

In order for me to do my daily work, I need his anointing, in order for me to reach the brokenhearted I need his anointing, in order for me to serve others the way that I should in spirit and in truth I need his anointing.

God's anointing can do things that man cannot do. I am constantly asking God for his miracles to be alive in my life. I am always asking God to help me succeed so that I will be able to help others. I am always asking God for those things which I know that only he can do. All of these things requires the anointing.

With God's anointing all of these things shall and will come to pass. I cannot be the person that God has ordained me to be without his anointing. I want to be anointed. I want people to recognize my anointing. I want people to feel the anointing on my life.

I want to be a child of God that does not need an introduction but that my life speaks for itself. In order to obtain this, it would take the anointing of God on my life to show from the inside out.

I've been around people before and just their presence alone makes you want to get to know them more. The more that I look into them I recognize that it is the anointing of God on their life.

That's the type of anointing that I want. People want to know what is so different about me and I will be able to share with them the love of God with the anointing that he has placed in my life. The anointing of God is something that I have yearned for and I have been able to receive.

In all honesty I can't say that I wake up every morning with this anointing on my life but even after being reminded of just how great it is I will strive to apply more of his anointing in everything that I do.

Even writing this makes me excited in just recognizing just how things will begin to open up and create a way for me just by having this anointing every day. Doors that are supposed to be open that has been closed for years will begin to be open with his anointing.

A sickness that has followed me or tried to attach itself to me has to set me free with the anointing of God. Anything that is not of him cannot prevail or reside with me as long as the anointing is with me.

I am overjoyed in knowing that the anointing of God will make a way.

The anointing of God will begin to cover me and protect me from any demons; any spirits that are not like him, that were assigned to me to destroy me will be cast down.

Romans Chapter 8, Verse 37 says that, "*...we are more than conquerors and gain a surpassing victory through him who loved us.*" This means that believers are empowered by God to have victory over sin and things in this world that try to keep us from following God's way.

The key to living in God's power is the anointing. The anointing of God's ability to assist you in knowing that you do not have to worry about anything and that there should be no struggle.

To live a life without the anointing is a life which is stagnated. In this scripture there are something's that we should keep close to our heart in reminding us that he has called us to do a work and we are anointed by him to do it, which at times may seem unbearable, butthe anointing is what allow us the ability to get them done.

The anointing is our strength.

First **John Chapter 2, Verse 20** says, you have been anointed by the holy one, means that he will provide for us. As long as we remain obedient the anointing will flow in our lives.

The anointing will flow in every area of our lives rather we are in church praying for a sister or brother, at the doctor's office expecting a miracle, or at work trying to meet deadlines we have been anointed for this moment.

It is imperative for us to know that God has given us the anointing to apply to our lives, and should so daily.

Chapter 6: The Authority

As a young child while growing up I always admired the work of the SWAT team members, the undercover agents, and the FBI. Although it wasn't appropriate for a five-year-old, I watched Beverly Hills Cops with Eddie Murphy as the main character over and over again and even practiced some of the scenes where he was busy trying to catch the bad guys.

Another one of my favorites was RoboCop, and the Terminator. I used the term, *"I'll be back"*, over and over again in real life and would say this phrase instead of saying the word goodbye to fellow family members, friends, and teachers.

Although this was learned behavior from the movies which I watched and studied, I never became a SWAT team member or anyone in law enforcement.

I was very serious about this career and even received an undergraduate degree in Criminal justice and I thought that I would become a police officer and work my way up.

Needless to say, this was never the career path that I actually chose after grad school but I recognize that in many ways I have become an agent for God. I've traded out running after the bad guys, drug dealers, and street thugs, and have begun to cast out demons and rebuke ungodly things.

People often use the phrase that God has a sense of humor and I can completely understand that in my line of work. I wanted something and he gave it to me in his likeness.

Be an Agent of God

As an agent of God, it is my duty to enforce the authority on earth that God has placed within me.

Do you recognize that according to the word of God the believer has complete authority over his realm of jurisdiction? As believers, we have the authority to command the devil out of the realm of our jurisdiction and to appoint or charge the elect angels to move on our behalf.

This authority was given to me to demand, decree and receive the things that I know belongs to me. This authority also was given to me to cast out demons and, to feel confident in knowing that I can remind the devil of his future in Jesus name.

The authority that has been given to us is not to be abused but to be used for the glory of

God. Just as God's word has stated this authority has been given to us under conditions and these conditions include, hearing the word of God, knowing the word of God, believing in the word of God, and acting on the word of God.

By applying this to my everyday life, I recognize that I have the authority to decree things into existence. I often grew up in church with people saying that it did not require a whole lot to praise God.

I equated that statement to meaning that I should not want overly nice things, because I would not be able to walk accordingly to God's word.

For years, I suffer from thinking having just enough was all intended for me not knowing that I had that authority to ask God for things, believe him for them, and watch them manifest in my life. When we were giving the authority to decree and declare, God was allowing us to speak into our futures, to call things to existence, and to demand that certain spirits exit our perimeter.

In **Galatians Chapter 4, Verse 7** the word reminds us and says, *"...we are no longer servants, but sons of God, and if we are sons then we are in his heirs. We are entitled to the inheritance that Christ has left us."*

What is this inheritance, you ask? Well, the inheritance is all about how you canuse your authority to decree success to come to pass. We have this authority, but this often goes unused.

This authority was designed for us to use, to step out and believe that we can have whatever our heart desires because we are the sons of God.

I'm not sure how I completely forgot about this considering that God has given us the power to cast out devils, speak with new

110

tongues, drink daily poison and take up serpents, not be harmed, and heal the sick by the laying of hands as stated in**Mark Chapter 16, Verses 17-18**.

If this is the word that God has left for us, then surely he can provide us with our needs according to the riches of his glory as stated in **Philippians Chapter 4, Verse 19**.

Many of our churches don't recognize that God want us to have the nice things in life. He also wants us to follow his word and by following his word we are able to ask for what we want and receive success.

It's sad to think that many Christians are living beneath their rights and privileges because they are not aware that they are sons of God and heirs to the inheritance that Christ has left for us.

We have the authority to ask and receive. We also have the authority to protect ourselves.

God has equipped us with the whole armor of God which we can use to fight against the wiles of the enemy as stated in **Ephesians Chapter 6, Verses 10-18**, *"Finally, be strong in the Lord and in his mighty power. Put on the full armor of God, so that you can take your stand against the devil's schemes.*

For our struggle is not against flesh and blood, but against the rulers, against the authorities, against the powers of this dark world and against the spiritual forces of evil in the heavenly realms.

Therefore put on the full armor of God, so that when the day of evil comes, you may be able to stand your ground, and after you have done everything, to stand. Stand firm then, with the belt of truth buckled around your waist, with the breastplate of righteousness in place, and with your feet fitted with the readiness that comes from the gospel of peace.

Yes God, I'm Listening!

In addition to all this, take up the shield of faith, with which you can extinguish all the flaming arrows of the evil one. Take the helmet of salvation and the sword of the Spirit, which is the word of God.

And pray in the Spirit on all occasions with all kinds of prayers and requests. With this in mind, be alert and always keep on praying for all of the Lord's people."

God has equipped us with everything that we need to be protected and to claim the victory. We must constantly remind ourselves that we have the victory and that we have already won through Jesus Christ. Until the people understand this fully Christians from all over the world will continue to live beneath certain standards thinking that they are following the word of God.

We were not intended to suffer for God. The suffering has already taken place on cavalry. We have the authority to demand our faith to be renewed and see the hand of the Lord in our lives.

God loved us so much, that he equipped us with all that we need. Have you have ever looked at your own life and recognized that your life is a product of what you believed you are worth? This thought should make you do one of two things: one, either continue to decree, declare, and petition God for your wants and needs, or two begin to decree and declare the life you want to exist for you. (Of course given with conditions only)

Chapter 7: Declaring your Faith in God

Having an understanding of spiritual authority is very vital in order to build upon your faith. We often ask God to bring the demonic forces out of someone when he has already given us the power and the tools to do this ourselves.

We have the authority over these demands, and we have the authority to decree that things be done on earth as it is in heaven. I think the mindset of many of us is to ask, to plead, or to beg Jesus to hear our cry, but what we keep forgetting is the authority has already been giving to us and we can use as a command to manifest things into our existence.

We are not told to ask God to please bring out demons we are told to cast them out and get it done. Our authority is demonstrated through the words that we speak.

The power of life and death are spoken in our words according to **Proverbs Chapter 18, Verse 21**which states " *death and life are in the power of the tongue.*" We have gained the authority through Jesus Christ then we shall be able to do all things.

Jesus was given the authority over everything according to Matthew Chapter 28, Verse 18, which states all powers given to me in heaven and in earth.

In all honesty, I'm not sure that we understood that the authority has been given to us to decree and to get things done. I think I have took it as asking God for the strength and the power and authority to do things in his name not knowing that he has already given me the okay to do so.

Yes God, I'm Listening!

When I pray I say things such as "in the name of Jesus please allow me" or "give me", which are all terms indicating that I am expecting him to give me something that I don't already have.

In recognizing that his authority abides in me, I am now able to decree that things are done and believe it as so. This is a new way of thinking for me and I am excited to know and very humble to understand my authority in Christ.

God's authority is not something to take lightly but to use to cast out demons, to heal the sick, and to heal a broken hearted world.

With this authority, we should now understand what we are expected to do and what we have the power to do. We should feel similar to the 70 disciples that God had given the authority to cast out demons which is found in **Luke Chapter 10, Verse 17**.

The scriptures read that the disciples were excited and joyful to share that even the devils were subject to the name of Jesus. The disciples did not recognize the authority they had been given was the authority to cast out, to demand, to decree, and to make it happen.

They were joyful in knowing that by using the name of Jesus everything had to come under subjection.

How will you begin to use your authority?

There is authority in the name of Jesus. **Revelations Chapter 1, Verse 18** reminds us that *"I am alive forever more and have the keys of hell and of death."* Jesus now has the authority forever more.

"All power and authority is given to me in heaven and on earth" according to **Matthew Chapter 28, Verse 18**.

Jesus then immediately delegated his authority to the sons of God in **Matthew**

118

Chapter 28, Verse 19 when he said, "*...go you, therefore, and these signs shall follow them that believe in my name.*" Therefore, we are the sons of God which he was referring to and now we have the authority to do the work of the Lord.

With this authority I plan to do exactly that and begin to recognize that I have the power and everything I need to get things done. I'm not going to say that I will never forget how powerful my authority is because I probably will forget at times. I'm not going to say that my authority sometimes will be diminished by issues and things I'm going through because it probably will.

At least now when I am reminded by the word of God about the authority that I possess I will begin to use it in a different mindset, a different way in understanding that God has already given me the authority that I need to trample over serpents and to decree certain things into existence.

Knowing I have this authority allows me the opportunity to use it accordingly to how God instructed me to use it, being able to walk with a different mindset in knowing that I have the power to overcome every obstacle, to cast out every demon, and to decree things into existence.

Ask and You Shall Receive

In **John Chapter 16, Verses 23-24**, states, *"Whatever you ask the father in my name he will give you. Until now you have asked nothing in my name. Ask and you will receive that your joy may be full."*

This scripture clearly describes exactly what I'm trying to say that I have not been able to use the authority in the way that it was intended to be used because I was not knowledgeable of the authority that I had.

Now that I have been made aware of this authority I would begin to use it more effectively in understanding that when I ask, and when I decree, that it shall be and all I would need to do is be patient.

Chapter 8: Establishing your Heavenly Identity

If you look up the true definition of identity on Wikipedia or any other dictionary, it defines identity as a person's conception an expression of their own and others individuality or a group affiliation.

It goes on to say that one may define identity as the distinctive characteristic belonging to any given individual are shared by all members of a particular social category our group.

Your identity is a label.

When I think of having a heavenly identity I think of living a life exactly to Christ. I think of walking, talking and representing him in every aspect of my life.

When I think of having a heavenly identity I know that flesh is not something that I would entertain because God was of the Spirit and of the spirit only.

The term heavenly identity reminds me of a heart of Christ which not only brings about deliverance but also set the captives free.

Walking in my heavenly identity means that I am no longer the same person. I no longer have the same walk, talk, or mindset.

My mind has been renewed and restored through Christ and I now walk in the power and the authority of Jesus Christ. I now have the mind of Christ walking in my heavenly identity.

1 Corinthians Chapter 2, Verse 16 says, *"for, who has known the mind of the Lordso as to instruct him?"*As I began to walk with my heavenly identity I will begin to receive results that I have never been able to see before.

I will be able to have a new revelation that has never been revealed to me before. I will now understand and see the true work of God in my life in all areas by having this heavenly perspective.

Colossians Chapter 3, Verses 1-4 says, *"If ye then be risen with Christ, seek those things which are above, where Christ sitteth on the right hand of God. Set your affection on things above, not on things on the earth. For ye are dead, and your life is hid with Christ in God. When Christ, who is our life, shall appear, then shall ye also appear with him in glory."*

These scriptures put the belief of heavenly identity in perspective and give you a clear description of life with Christ. It's Awesome to see and be reminded that when Jesus was resurrected from the dead we as a people meaning his children were raised with him.

From this point on we were giving the opportunity to walk in our heavenly identity. The word reminds us to set our hearts on things above where Christ is seated at the right hand of God therefore not taking anything on Earth too serious but knowing that our treasures are in heaven.

It gives us the opportunity to see that earth is not our final destination and we should not worry about things which are out of our control here on earth because there is a heavenly force which will guide us.

Matthew Chapter 6, Verses 19-21 says, *"Do not store up for you treasures on earth, where moths and vermin destroy, and where thieves break in and steal. But store up for you treasures in heaven, where moths and vermin do not destroy, and where thieves do not break in and steal.For where your treasure is, there your heart will be also."*

Dr. Shanta Barton-Stubbs

There is no need to worry about what you
don't possess here because in heaven is
where the true treasure lies.

126

Walk with God in your Heavenly Identity

Walking in our heavenly identity will help us avoid some of the chaos and drama that we often would encounter when walking in the flesh. Walking in our heavenly identity is keeping us fully equipped with the whole armor of God so that we can fight against every wile of the enemy.

Ephesians Chapter 6, Verse 11 states, *"Put on the full armor of God, so that you can take your stand against the devil's schemes."* This same chapter goes on to tell us that for our struggle is not against flesh and blood, but against the rulers, against the authorities, against the powers of this dark world and against the spiritual forces of evil in the heavenly realms.

With our heavenly identity, we are equipped to fight against these forces and claim victory in Jesus' name.

Walking in our heavenly identity would allow us to perform healings and see the signs and wonders of Christ's work through us.

I'm not sure how one can actually walk in their heavenly identity and experience a whole new life and then return back to walking in the flesh. There's no comparison between the heavenly identities versus the flesh.

In our heavenly identity all things are possible because of God just as it is mentioned in **Matthew Chapter 19, Verse 26**, in our flesh nothing is possible. In our heavenly identity, we have power over the flesh.

Romans Chapter 8, Verse 9 says, *"You, however, are not in the realm of the flesh but*

Yes God, I'm Listening!
are in the realm of the Spirit, if indeed the
Spirit of God lives in you. And if anyone
does not have the Spirit of Christ, they do
not belong to Christ."

You, however, are not in the realm of the flesh but are in the realm of the Spirit; if indeed the Spirit of God lives in you. Walking in our heavenly identity gives us the power to do things we have never done before.

It allows us to see God in a whole new way since he is now living within us. Walking in the spirit of God makes the flesh obsolete to us unless we allow the flesh to come in.

I was thinking that in order to have a heavenly identity what must I do? It seems to be a process when thinking about it in the natural.

I can think back of being a marine for a short amount time and needing to prepare for months physically and mentally to get ready for the transition. I think it was more mentally than anything. I thought about it before I acted it out. Walking in the identity of Christ one must renew themselves as mentioned before, let go of our own ways, and follow Christ.

In order to walk in my heavenly identity, I recognized that it was a lot like preparing for the Marines but in a spiritual sense. I need to constantly set my mind on the things of the spirit.

In order to maintain my heavenly identity, I must constantly feed my spirit and have my mind set on things which are of the Spirit just as **Colossians Chapter 3** states, *"Since, then, you have been raised with Christ, set your hearts on things above, where Christ is, seated at the right hand of God. Set your minds on things above, not on earthly things.*

Yes God, I'm Listening!

For you died, and your life is now hidden with Christ in God. When Christ, who is your life, appears, then you also will appear with him in glory.Put to death, therefore, whatever belongs to your earthly nature: sexual immorality, impurity, lust, evil desires and greed, which is idolatry...

Because of these, the wrath of God is coming. You used to walk in these ways, in the life you once lived. But now you must also rid yourselves of all such things as these: anger, rage, malice, slander, and filthy language from your lips. Do not lie to each other, since you have taken off your old self with its practices and have put on the new self, which is being renewed in knowledge in the image of its Creator.

Here there is no Gentile or Jew, circumcised or uncircumcised, barbarian, Scythian, slave or free, but Christ is all, and is in all."

Therefore, as God's chosen people, holy and dearly loved, clothe yourselves with compassion, kindness, humility, gentleness and patience. Bear with each other and forgive one another if any of you has a grievance against someone. Clean yourself of all fleshy ways, and take on the attributes of Christ.

Being an Ambassador of Christ

Forgive as the Lord forgave you. And over all these virtues put on love, which binds them all together in perfect unity. Let the peace of Christ rule in your hearts, since as members of one body you were called to peace. And be thankful.

Let the message of Christ dwell among you richly as you teach and admonish one another with all wisdom through psalms, hymns, and songs from the Spirit, singing to God with gratitude in your hearts.

And whatever you do, whether in word or deed, do it all in the name of the Lord Jesus, giving thanks to God the Father through him.It is only then that I will be living as those who are made alive in Christ.This means not letting evil, wickedness or any other negative forces enter into my mindset but using the word of God to combat spirits along with others.

Romans Chapter 8, Verse 5 also reminds us *"For those who live according to the flesh set their minds on the things of the flesh, but those who live according to the Spirit set their minds on the things of the Spirit."*

We must keep our mind focused on Christ and of things of the spirit in order to protect this identity.

In everyday life, it is so easy to be caught up into things which are not of Christ. Drama is around every corner and if you allow yourself to be assumed in it, you will eventually recognize that you have begun to walk in the flesh and become someone totally different from whom you strive to be.

I have found myself in this situation over and over again especially when surrounding myself with flesh minded people. It is very important for me to hold onto my identity in God and know who's I AM and what I represent.

I am an ambassador of Christ and should always walk as such.

2 Corinthians Chapter 5, Verse 20 reminds us that *"We are therefore Christ's ambassadors, as though God were making his appeal through us."* We represent Christ when we begin to walk in our heavenly identity.

According to **Isaiah Chapter 54, Verse 17**, *"No weapon that is formed against thee shall prosper"*, so I must have the confidence in knowing that I can conquer all things in my heavenly identity. I must continue to walk in the authority of knowing who I am and what I stand for.

No one can take me out of my identity unless I allow them to. I have to be more strong minded in understanding that my identity should be my DNA, it should be what I stand for, and it should be what I live for.

No other spirit in my DNA that does not belong to me should be able to overtake me or my mindset.

The word of God tells us that we are the sons of God which means that we should resemble Christ himself in the way that we present ourselves, the way that we talk, and the way that we live our everyday lives.

Our identity should be similar to that of Christ, just as it is in the natural with our biological parents. With our biological parents, we all have some resemblances. Either we look like our father, our mother and other family members; we received our looks from somebody.

Often times I am constantly told that I look like and resemble my mother. I am even told that I walk in some of the same anointing that she does. I never really thought about the fact that it's not that I'm walking in her same anointing, but we are similar because we are walking in the same identity of Christ. Christians should resemble one another. Yes, we will all have our own special gifts, but our spirit man should resemble one another since we are all confessing to have the identity of Christ.

Our heavenly identity represents that of Christ and everything that we do. Anyone who knows the Spirit of God and the word of God would understand that our spirit man's bear witness with one another and, therefore, resembles the life of Christ.

The more I become in tune with God and build my relationship with him the more people tell me *"I am walking more in the attributes of my mother."* Now I know how to respond in sharing that my heavenly identity is showing through my life just as it does for my mother.

If we are all walking with the mind of Christ in our heavenly identity then we all will talk the same, speak the word the same and share these resemblance since there is only one God to live our life after. We may all have different anointing but there should be something that resonates with people and that is the identity of Christ.

The more we walk in our heavenly identity the more we resemble Christ.

I get so excited in knowing that my walk should reflect that of Christ. This means there is nothing that I cannot do without him and with him I can do all things.

There are many times when I am asked to speak at different events sometimes which are not related to church. I often think on those things which I should say and ask God to lead me and guide me in saying the right things.

At times, I fear not knowing if my message will get across to the people. Many times people come to me afterwards and tell me that they can see Christ living through me although I did not use any biblical terms or did not clearly state the name of Jesus. Amazing how my heavenly identity can even show during messages such as this.

Walking in the heavenly identity requires thinking about your actions and your daily walk with God. It requires knowing that you are a son of God, and, therefore, must walk like you are.

Walking in the heavenly identity requires preparation of constantly equipping yourself with the word of God and walking therein. We have to grow into the spiritual man which we were born into. "*I am a spirit being born of God to conduct myself spiritually in the spirit realm."*

As we begin to seek God and become stronger we will begin to learn the effective way of walking in the heavenly identity. The more we began to walk in our heavenly identity we will recognize that it is more abnormal to walk in the flesh, as a spiritual being.

Ultimately I recognized that even in today's society there are many people who are of certain age but are not mature as one would expect them to be.

It's the same thing in Christ people can accept God into their life but don't feed their spirit man as it needs to be fed in order to gain maturity. In my own life I can see where I have accepted God, I have read the word, I have prayed and fast but have not been consistent as I should in order to say that I am walking in my heavenly identity.

There is no half way walk in God it's either walking upright or not walking with him at all.

Walking in the heavenly identity is not something that can be done part of the time, some of the time but should be done all of the time. My mindset needs to be changed to grasp this concept that this is not an identity that I can pick up and put down when I get ready, but must walk therein day and night.

To this day, I cannot say that I have honestly walked in my heavenly identity the way that I should have.

I can't even say that I have been consistent with the same walk on a day to day basis, but I do know that I have strived to be the best that I can be. I can see where I have let limitations control me and have been forced to think that certain things are good enough for me.

I can truly say that I have not yet walked in my full potential and have recognized this by becoming aware of the word of God in this lesson. I have not reached out to enjoy my life in Christ as much as I could have. I do believe that walking in a heavenly identity will:

1. **Assist me in becoming more willing to rely on the word of God and not my own understanding.**

2. **Help me understand that I am not in this walk alone, but I do have Christ and the word to help guide me along the way.**

3. **Walking in my heavenly identity is something that I can do on a daily basis and once I begin to do more of this it will become more**

of a second nature to me rather than me trying all inability to follow the word of God.

Knowing that I'm walking upright and pleasing God gives me satisfaction in knowing that I am living according to my purpose.

I don't want to go back, and I won't go back, but I would use this lesson as a way to apply to my everyday life and even remind my body, my mind, and my soul that we all would line up and walk in the dignity of Christ.

I am grateful for having the understanding that I now attain. I know that this identity is a part of my DNA and will be put into perspective and followed. I can do nothing on my own but with Christ I can do all things.

Think for a moment how would you continue to walk in your Heavenly Identity?

While I have always encouraged all the young people who come to me for assistance in their lives to pray to God as a way of communicating with him, I encourage you as well. Below I share a prayer which can be recited when you feel that you are not walking in your true identity.

While I cannot force you into reciting this, you could always come up with a prayer of your own whenever you feel you need to communicate with God.

Dear God,

Thank you for giving me the opportunity to understand my true identity in you. Thank you for sharing your blood on cavalry that is now the blood that runs through my veins.

The DNA that I possess I know now that is not my own but is of you. Help me to walk in my heavenly identity every day in all that I say and do. Guide my footsteps and my life in the way that you have planned for me.

Change my mindset into understanding that in your identity all things are possible. Assist me in understanding that there are no limitations in you. God, I need you to direct me and show me my life the way you have attended for me to live it.

Any identity that is not of you that has caused me to walk contrary to my heavenly identity I asked that it is renounced and sent back to the pits of hell.

I renounce any erroneous lifestyles, doctrines and mindsets that I have walked in that have not been of you.

I decree that my mind, body and soul began to line up with the word of God and that I begin to walk in the heavenly identity according to my father which art in heaven.

Amen.

Chapter 9: The Wisdom of the Holy Spirit

God has given all who accept him into their life spiritual gifts. These gifts are what we are to use in order to walk in the Spirit.

These gifts are also designed for the perfecting of the saints, for the work of the ministry, and for the edification of the body of Christ. These gifts are given to us not for us to keep personally but for the benefit of others.

Although we may want to walk in many gifts, God gives each gift to whomsoever he pleases.

1 Corinthians Chapter 12, Verse 7-11 states, "*...now to each one the manifestation of the Spirit is given for the common good. To one there, is given through the Spirit a message of wisdom, to another a message of* *knowledge by means of the same spirit, to another faith by the same spirit, to another gift of healing by that one spirit, to another miraculous powers, to another prophecy, to another distinguishing between spirits, to another speaking in different kinds of tongues and still to another the interpretation of tongues.*

All these are the work of one in the same spirit and he distributes them to each one just as he determines."

This helps us to recognize that the gifts which are given unto us were chosen by God and bestowed upon us as he sees the abilities in us. He will equip what is needed after giving us this gift as long as we continue to seek his word and grow in him.

In God, we can find all Things

1 Corinthians Chapter 2, Verse 5 states, *"...your faith should not stand in the wisdom of man but in the power of God."* Knowing that our gifts are giving to us by the Spirit of God then we can begin to walk in them and use them accordingly to see miracles performed.

Romans Chapter 15, Verse 19 says, we are reminded that in the power of signs and wonders lies the power of the Spirit.

So without the Holy Spirit you cannot flow in the anointing of God, we would not be able to have the power to show signs and wonders without the Spirit of God. The Holy Spirit is only available when we have completely yielded ourselves onto God and have become free from certain emotions, and negative thoughts which come against who God is and what he can do.

The Holy Spirit will lead us pass any of our erroneous thoughts and unrealistic thinking.

The Holy Spirit does not exist around doubt or disbelief. This is a clear direction for us Christians to understand in order to receive or to see miracles take place we must believe in the Holy Spirit and it must be present in our lives.

I can now see why the enemy would fight very hard to keep us from remaining in the Spirit of God because he knows that in the Spirit of God all things are possible. In the spirit of God, we are able to do the impossible.

I know that the word of God will come true in our life. The Holy Spirit is the gift which is given unto us to walk into miracles and to see them take place. There's no way that negativity and the Holy Spirit can reside in the same spirit man.

In order to see miracles come to pass the Holy Spirit, must be present. The Holy Spirit is our comforter.

This is the gift that God has given us to let us know that he has everything in control if we allow him to work through us through the Holy Spirit. Jesus himself cannot come to earth and live through us and hence, this is why he sent the Holy Spirit to be our comforter and guide us.

John Chapter 14, Verse 15-27 reminds us how to keep the command of God and to also recognize the gift which he has left with us and is living through us through the Holy Spirit. It is very important for us to recognize that the Holy Spirit is the guide that will lead us to all truth.

It is impossible to follow God unless we are led by the Holy Spirit, and the only way to be led by the Spirit is to follow God's command, to be filled by the Spirit according to

Ephesians Chapter 5, Verse 18 which states, *"Do not get drunk on wine, which leads to debauchery, and instead be filled with the Spirit."*

To be filled with the spirit is the command that God has left us. In order to walk in the authority in the anointing of God, the Holy Spirit must be present.

This is a great reminder for me who constantly at times appear to not understand the walk that I am walking in its entirety. There is no way to walk in the spirit but yet have feelings of unbelief for doubt which sometimes happens when crucial or crisis situations come alive in my life.

I have to choose which one I plan to walk in either in the spirit in doubt.

Romans Chapter 8, Verse 5 states, *"Those who live according to the flesh have their minds set on what the flesh desires; but* *those who live in accordance with the spirit have their minds set on what the spirit desires."*

My reminder is that either I am walking in the flesh or I am walking in the Spirit. If I am walking in the flesh that means my mind is not set on those things of God if I am walking in the Spirit and I am allowing myself to hear the word of God, and yielding myself to the Spirit of God, I can walk therein.

In order for us to cooperate with the Holy Spirit to see miracles happen we must constantly walk in the spirit. Letting go of all other mindsets, thoughts, things or even people who walk contrary to the word of God should be our main mission when walking in Christ.

The Holy Spirit is a comforter and there have been numerous times when I have turned to the Holy Spirit to help me get through the trials and tribulations of life.

For even when things seem out of control this comforter spirit is there to keep my mind on God and knowing that he will prevail and that his word would not come back void. I am learning that the Holy Spirit is the "Jesus living in me".

Since Jesus was not able to be here himself with us he sent himself through the spirit of God.

We must learn to live and walk in the Spirit of God in order to maintain the relationship that we have with God. The Holy Spirit would not lead us wrong because the Holy Spirit cannot walk in the flesh.

When I find myself walking in the flesh or doing things contrary to the word of God I now know I must check myself and recognize that I am not walking in the Holy Spirit which has been bestowed upon me.

Yes God, I'm Listening!

The Holy Spirit can perform miracles in our lives. Without the Holy Spirit, miracles cannot be performed this is something that we must constantly remind ourselves of. Every day we should invite the Holy Spirit in and allow him to walk with us.

I would not want to continue a day without the Holy Spirit. A day without the Holy Spirit is almost like a day walking blind, but now that I have become knowledgeable in knowing that the Holy Spirit is my guide, I must walk with this anointing daily.

There is no way that I would want to live a day without the Holy Spirit. The Holy Spirit was my special gift that God gave me when I accepted him into my life.

Honestly, I cannot say that I walk in the Holy Spirit on a daily basis. There are times where the Spirit is around. I feel him. I see him. I recognized him, but there are other times where I have allowed situations doubts feelings and things to come into my mind and allow me to walk into a different mindset.

No wonder things began to spin out of control because now I am no longer covered under the Spirit of God but under an actual spirit. Ugh, but that's for another book.

Applying the Wisdom of the Holy Spirit

Applying the Holy Spirit to my everyday life will help me see the fruits of my labor, and the inheritance that God has left for me. I can see and recognize that the Spirit of God would take me and give me those things that my heart desire. I can also see where and I have not received those things mainly due to me walking with spirits which were not of Christ.

If Christ should reflect a certain lifestyle, then surely there are times when I can look back and see that the spirit which I was walking in was not the Holy Spirit. Can we all be honest with ourselves? What does our life reflect? Are people able to see the attributes of Christ in our lives?

Behold the Lamb of God now that I recognize my gift from God and know how to apply it I will begin to walk in the spirit not only to inherit the things that God has left for me but also to help other people become free.

The more you meditate on the word the greater the anointing becomes on your life. There are a lot of people who call themselves anointed but you know whether they are or not by the fruit that they bear.

This appears to be basic logic and knowing that the more you seek God's word the more you begin to walk in the way of the word. As Christians, we know this but yet we allow so many other things to get in our way to keep us from the word of God.

I can speak for myself and have recognized that even writing this I have become stronger, more knowledgeable and more willing to be used by God by getting more of the word in me on a daily basis.

Why would I not want this anointing on my life knowing that this anointing could give me my every heart desire and give me the life that I know God has destined for me? Why would I want to go back to barely having or just enough when I have experienced life with Christ?

The more that I study I recognize that my walk with God becomes stronger and I'm learning to decree things and seeing them happen. There's no way that I would experience this and allow the flesh to step in and go about life the way I have been going about it all these many years.

Only a fool would experience Christ to this extent and turn back to a fleshly way. I am no fool, and I know that the word that I am now consuming is causing the anointing on my life to be present and it's showing in everything that I'm doing. In order for me to walk fully in the life of Christ, I must not only have this anointing some of the time but must maintain it on a regular basis in order to help other people also be delivered.

I have found that in the past so many times I have become discouraged and have taken my eyes off of God.

I have recognized that this is a tactic from the enemy to bind me and to get my mind off of heavenly things. A fleshly mindset will begin to think about things which are not taking place the way you have prayed for them to take place.

A mind of Christ will remind your spirit man about the word of God and what God has

159

promised. God's promises will come to pass. Now if only I can begin to apply this to my own life and recognize that miracles signs and wonders are only present when I am walking in the anointing of God.

When I am walking in the flesh miracles signs and wonders would not be performed. It appears to be a simple equation, but so hard to apply when not walking therein or when not experiencing God the way you feel you should.

Being Anointed by the Holy Ghost

When you're anointed by the Holy Ghost you are not considered normal. When other people give up that's when you kick in. I have questioned this for many years and wondered why I appeared to be so different from others who are professing Christ just as I am.

I have tried for many years to even fit in and recognized that no matter what I did I always stood out. I'm not a person who gives up, I'm not a person who gives in, I'm not a person who throws in the towel, I'm a person who would go to the end until the job is completed and done.

Now I recognize that the anointing in me is what pushes me to be this way and pushes me to achieve the goals which are set out for me. The anointing on my life will not allow me to give up because I continue to cultivate my anointing on a daily basis by praying, fasting, and remaining in my word.

If there was ever a time when I no longer cultivated this relationship then I would be more vulnerable to giving up and being considered mediocre. Mediocre people give up, mediocre people do just enough to get by.

Mediocre people don't push past their comfort zone and are willing to settle for what's in front of them. This is the life of people who don't walk in the supernatural powers which God has given us. On many cases I have found myself feeling sorry for mediocre people because I want to see them enjoy the inheritance of God, but they have to want it for themselves as bad as I want it for them.

It is my job as a woman of God to assist them in where they should be, but they have to want it just as bad and be willing to work for it and obey the word of God.

In order to maintain the fresh anointing on my life, I must have fresh oil daily. I need a stirring and a refill in my life daily to remain strong for a victorious living.

When not performing at my best, I must seek God for a refueling, and recognize my deficiencies rather than going through the motions. When going through the motions, I am doing myself unjust, and not being refueled as needed.

The power of God will allow me to stand up when needed and to tell the truth rather I want to be heard or not. The anointing of God is alive in my life if I allow it to be. We all fall short and become weak, but the supernatural powers of Christ will renew us.

The source of my richness is the result of the power of God. I must know the meaning of my anointing. I can't say that I always knew the meaning of my anointing, but I have always known that the anointing was present in my life. I have always known that I have not been like any other person.

With my anointing, I must guard it and be aware of when I need to be refueled.

Walking in supernatural powers is God's plan for me. For me to live and inherit the blessings that he has stored for me.

The Bible says in **Hebrews Chapter 10, Verse 38**, "*But my righteous one will live by faith. I take no pleasure in the one who shrinks back.*" In order to be a part of the remnant which will be used mightily by God, you must be willing to press toward the mark which is the high calling.

God gets no satisfaction in the person who does just enough and doesn't press towards being greater as mentioned above. This means that we as the sons of God should press hard, not give up, be more dedicated and more willing than others.

We will never arrive at our full potential without some discipline, without some trials, and without issues, so we must prepare for them. This is what pushes me to be better and stronger in God.

Prayer, the Answer to Everything!

Constant prayer, constant fasting, and constant pushing is the formula to be successful in God which will also show up in your life. So many times people wait day after day for things to happen, instead of using today as the day to get started.

The scriptures says in **Psalm 18, Verse 24**, that this is the day that the Lord has made; let us rejoice and be glad in it. This is the day, today is the day to begin and walk therein.

The longer you wait the longer your blessings will be prolonged; the longer it takes for you to reach success, the longer it takes for you to grow in God.

The longer you wait the more days you waste and there is no way to make up the days

166

which you have wasted. Every day counts towards pushing for better and allowing the supernatural powers to work through you.

When we came to Christ we came to Christ as a baby, a baby Christian. God has given us the supernatural powers to grow and to become who God has called us to be.

Stagnation is of the enemy and is a sign that a person is not using their supernatural powers to grow up. Christians should show progress in their life and we should see the work of God in all that we do.

It is not okay for you to be in one situation one year and find yourself in the same situation year after year. It comes a time when you must activate your supernatural powers and begin to show growth in all areas of your life.

No change is defined as a lack of progress, a lack of supernatural powers in your life. Or should we say the lack of applying those supernatural powers to your life. It is our choice, do you believe that?

It's our choice to activate this power or deny it. This means we should not complain about life when it gives us certain results because some of the results we actually manifested for ourselves.

When you stay stagnated, it's because you have become double minded and not willing to separate yourself from mediocre people, negative thoughts or erroneous doctrines.

Anyone can reach little goals, but it takes the supernatural powers to see the move of God in your life, to go after bigger goals.

Anyone can set goals which can be accomplished by the week, but it takes only a person of destiny to go beyond what they feel and reach for something that appears next to impossible to reach.

A person of destiny doesn't see the current situation but focuses on the final outcome. God has given us the power and we are now sons of God. A son of God is a person who is destroying the work of the devil.

When the work of the enemy is destroyed then the powers began to work within your life. A person of destiny knows the importance of these powers and how to execute them daily.

The Bible tells us in **Isaiah Chapter 1, Verse 19** that we must be willing and obedient to the work of God in order to enjoy the fruits of the land.

In order to be blessed we must be both willing and obedient. One without the other would not produce the work of God. It is so important for us to understand on a daily basis that our life does not belong to us but we must be obedient to the word of God and willing to do the work which he has called us to do.

Many people are not willing to be obedient to the word of God and do the work which he has called them to do and therefore you see a lot of Christians not producing. We have to be willing to believe and walk in the word of God daily.

Our Supernatural powers are active when we pray to God honestly, worship with him whole heartily and, follow the word of God.

As I stated in the previous chapter, I tend to pray a lot and often because there is nothing comparable to a prayer which comes from the heart of a human being than from the mind.

Never ever force yourself into prayer. Nobody appreciates a forced conversation and same rules apply for a prayer.

My prayer below is what came to me while thinking about how I could explain myself clearly to you in this chapter, how the Holy Spirit when called upon helps calm the mind and soul.

My Personal Prayer

Dear God,

After recognizing that I have not lived accordingly to your word, and have not inherited all that you have in store for me I am coming to you for forgiveness and most importantly direction.

There's no way that I can become aware and knowledgeable of the vision that you have for my life and not want to walk in it.

Although I have evaluated my life and have recognized several key areas which have allowed me to walk contrary to my divine purpose I ask you to also identify other areas that I need to address and become more aware of in order for me to be the best that I need to be in you.

Rather that contains people, situations, thought patterns, or even generational curses I pray that you began to show me the changes that I need to make in order to be the woman of God you have called me to be.

My prayer has always been, Lord to bless me with enough so that I can help other people but I am now able to see that this is already in your word and in order for me to truly walk in you I must recognize the supernatural powers that you have given me to walk in.

I must also recognize the spiritual gifts and talents that you have given to me and begin to use them for your glory. Forgive me for acting like an immature Christian, and a baby Christian in so many areas. I want you to know, I hear you God, and yes I am listening!

I am now willing to be obedient to the word of God and willing to do the work that you have designed for me. I know that I have not been all bad but I want to be 100% for you. Allow my mind and my walk, and talk to reflect you.

Give me the reminders that I need on a daily basis to activate my super natural powers to help others as well as achieve the success that I was destined for. Thank you for the word which has been imparted in my heart, my mind and my soul and thank you for IMI for being the source of which I have learned the true meaning of my relationship with you.

Continue to surround me with awesome great people who will continue to pour into me the word of God and teach me how to reach the levels in you that I need to continue to grow in.

Thank you for anointing me to be the woman of God that I am and the woman of God that I will continue to grow to be. I pray that the power of the supernatural began to follow me and began to show forth in everything that I do.

I have asked for forgiveness and now I'm willing to walk according to what I have learned. Assist me in applying the word to my everyday life and be the example of Christ that I want to be.

Allow my soul to yearn for you and never to look back. Allow me to use this Doctoral degree as a way to reach others and to also share the things that I have learned with others in order to see them be set free.

Please guide my heart, my mind, my soul and the things that I say so that they would edify the word of God in all that I do. Allow my life to be an example of what it is to live with Christ fully.

Yes God, I'm Listening!

Thank you God for choosing me.

Thank you God for directing me to this point in my life as I continue to touch a dying world.

Equip me with the strength and the encouragement that I need to continue to go on in you in Jesus name.

Amen.

Chapter 10: Important Daily Reminders

Know Thyself by Knowing God

- God has given me the authority to decree things into existence. God's plan for my life is to be successful and to enjoy the inheritance he has left me.

- God has given me the anointing to heal the sick to heal the brokenhearted and to cast out demons.

- God already has a plan for my life, but it is up to me to decide which life I choose to walk in.

-The only way to identify with Christ is through the word of God.

-My spiritual relationship with God will grow in proportion to my faith.

-Nothing will stop the flow of God in my life quicker than doubt and unbelief.

-The words that I speak determine the life that I live.

Reality Check: Get back to those things which I was called to do

Conclusion

I would like to conclude my book with a Thank You! Thank you for reading this book and walking with me and Our Heavenly Father.

While you would have had certain enlightening moments in this book, I believe we cannot all be perfect, I certainly am not perfect and I don't think I will ever achieve the perfection I aim for. But on the other hand, my faith has taught me to accept myself, flaws and everything.

By accepting my own flaws, I will be able to accept flaws in other folks too and this makes our relationships grow stronger.

In **Romans Chapter 2, Verse 1**, the Bible says, *"Therefore you have no excuse, O man, every one of you who judges. For in passing judgment on another you condemn yourself,*

Yes God, I'm Listening!
because you, the judge, practice the very same things."

While it is difficult for us as humans to be able to control our tongues as well as our actions, we need to understand that when we walk with Christ and God his father, we need to be able to depict Christ like behavior.

My book is not intended to be a preachy one instead I would like to reach out to many of you through this book. I like to share what I have experienced in my life and on a daily basis on my journey with God. And Simply teach others, how to say Yes God, I'm listening.

It is only fair that I speak about my true experiences and even the times I have faltered along the way by being weak in my faith in God and his wondrous ways of working miracles in my life.

James Chapter 1, Verse 6, aptly sums up what I would like to say to end this book on my 'Walk with God'.

The verse in the Bible states, *"But when you ask, you must believe and not doubt, because the one who doubts is like a wave of the sea, blown and tossed by the wind."*

Dear friend, we can only walk with God and his beloved Son, Jesus if we believe in the plan for us.

Remember, when you shine bright, it is the reflection of Christ that others around you are witnessing and this is what brings glory galore to our Lord and Savior.

Wishing youa joyful walk with God in faith and love.

Don't forget to let God know you are listening! He is always willing to hear from you.